Arctic National

Wildlife Refuge

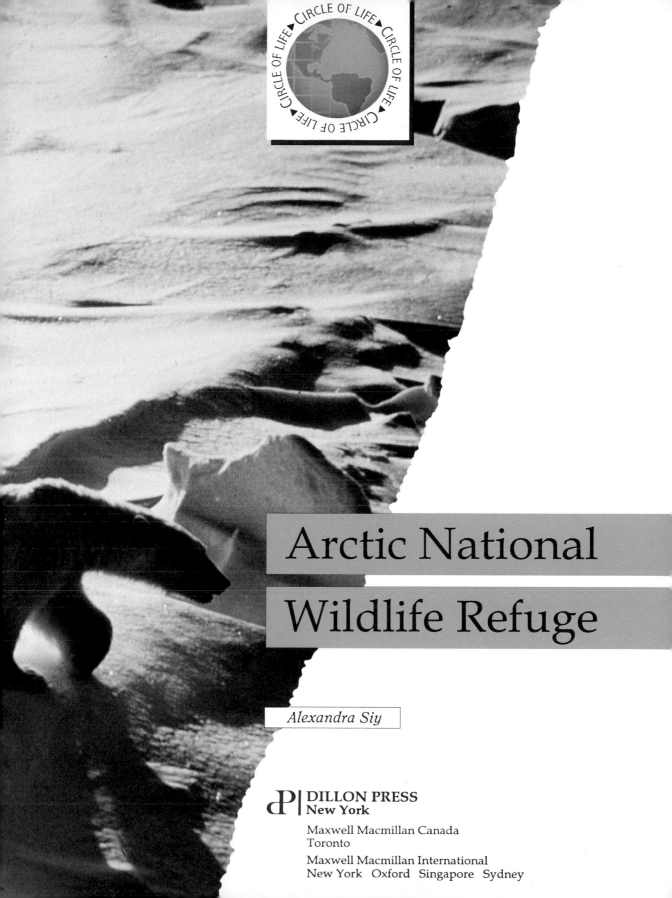

CIRCLE OF LIFE ▶ CIRCLE OF LIFE ▶ CIRCLE OF LIFE ▶ CIRCLE OF LIFE ▶ CIRCLE OF LIFE

Arctic National
Wildlife Refuge

Alexandra Siy

dP | DILLON PRESS
New York

Maxwell Macmillan Canada
Toronto

Maxwell Macmillan International
New York Oxford Singapore Sydney

For my brothers:
Peter of Alaska, and Matthew, Jim, and John of the lower forty-eight

Acknowledgments

I would like to thank the Wilderness Society of Alaska and the National Wildlife Federation of Alaska for providing information. Thanks also go to Janet Christiansen, botanist for the Arctic National Wildlife Refuge; Rob Lipkin, botanist for the Alaska Natural Heritage Program; and Pamela Bangart of the Yukon Executive Council Office for contributing information.

Thanks also go to John G. Rogers and Lavonda Walton of the U.S. Fish and Wildlife Service for providing photographs, and to Mary Lou Grinwis of the Elizabethtown, New York, library for helping me obtain reference materials.

I would also like to thank my brother, Peter Roberts, of Anchorage, Alaska, for contributing suggestions and information.

Photographic Acknowledgments

The photographs are reproduced through the courtesy of NASA; U.S. Department of Agriculture; U.S. Fish and Wildlife Service: B. Anderson, Gerry Atwell, Jim Clark, Jerry Hout, Jo Keller, Fran Mauer, Jan Nickles, Brian O'Donnell, Dave Olson, Jill Parker, Jerald Stroebele, Hans Stuart and Steve Warble.

Library of Congress Cataloging-in-Publication Data

Siy, Alexandra.
   Arctic National Wildlife Refuge/ by Alexandra Siy.
      p. cm. — (A Circle of life book)
   Includes index.
    Summary: Explores the plant and animal life found in the Arctic National Wildlife Refuge on the Alaskan tundra.
   ISBN 0-87518-468-5
    1. Tundra ecology—Alaska—Arctic National Wildlife Refuge—Juvenile literature. 2. Natural history—Alaska—Arctic National Wildlife Refuge—Juvenile literature. 3. Arctic National Wildlife Refuge (Alaska)—Juvenile literature. [1. Natural history—Alaska. 2. Tundra ecology. 3. Ecology. 4. Arctic National Wildlife Refuge (Alaska)] 1. Title. II. Series.
QH105. A4S59 1991
574. 9798' 7—dc20   91-3882

Dillon Press
Macmillan Publishing Company
866 Third Avenue
New York, NY 10022

Maxwell Macmillan Canada, Inc.
1200 Eglinton Avenue East
Suite 200
Don Mills, Ontario M3C 3N1

Macmillan Publishing Company is part of the Maxwell Communication Group of Companies.
First edition

Printed in the United States of America
10   9   8   7   6   5   4   3   2   1

Contents

▼

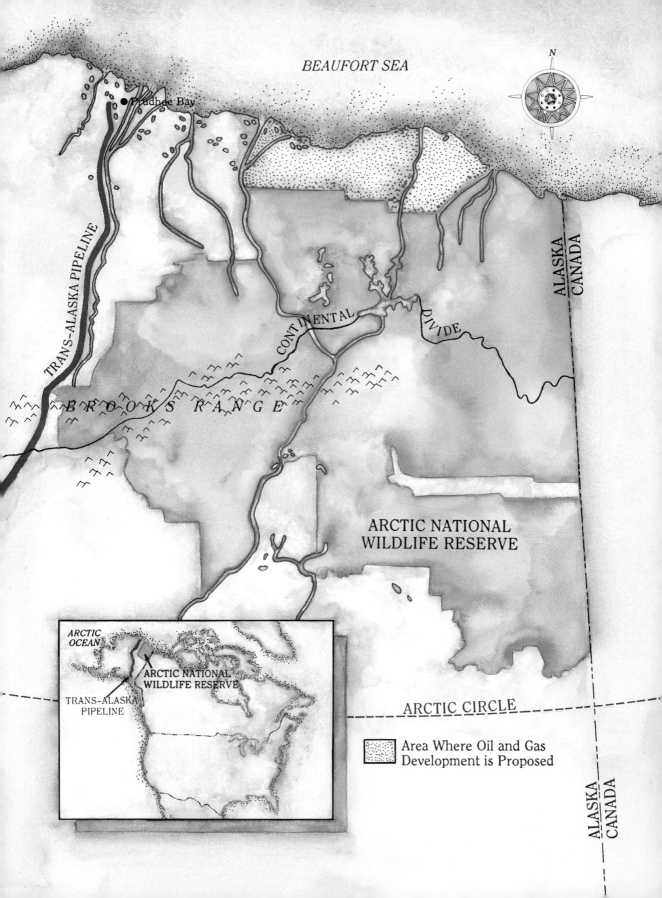

BEAUFORT SEA

N

Prudhoe Bay

TRANS-ALASKA PIPELINE

CONTINENTAL

DIVIDE

ALASKA
CANADA

B R O O K S   R A N G E

ARCTIC NATIONAL
WILDLIFE RESERVE

ARCTIC
OCEAN

ARCTIC NATIONAL
WILDLIFE RESERVE

TRANS-ALASKA
PIPELINE

ARCTIC CIRCLE

Area Where Oil and Gas
Development is Proposed

ALASKA
CANADA

▼

Facts

Location: The Arctic National Wildlife Refuge covers nineteen million acres of northeastern Alaska and includes lands north of the Arctic Circle.

Geography: The Arctic National Wildlife Refuge includes the northern forests south of the Brooks Mountain Range and the arctic tundra to the north. The northern coastal plain is the last remaining stretch of Alaskan coastline (125 out of 1,060 miles) along the Arctic Ocean that has not been developed.

Geology: The arctic was the final place from which the glaciers of the last ice age melted. Left behind was the tundra, a treeless land where plants grow close to the ground.

Climate: The arctic tundra has very cold winter temperatures (averaging below 0°F) and short, cool summers. Year-round precipitation is low—about four to sixteen inches a year.

Human History: The Inuit people have lived in Alaska's arctic for about ten thousand years. They have made a living by hunting and fishing over large areas of tundra. Alaska became the forty-ninth state in 1959.

Human Way of Life: Small villages of Inuit people exist near the Arctic National Wildlife Refuge. Some still hunt the caribou for food and clothing. In recent years, the discovery of oil on Alaska's north slope has provided many Alaskans with jobs.

Global Importance: The Arctic National Wildlife Refuge is the last place in the world where a complete arctic ecosystem has been left untouched by human development. The coastal plain supports many kinds of wildlife, including the largest herd of caribou on earth and migrating birds from all over the world.

Current Status: The coastal plain is threatened by oil development. The U.S. Congress must decide whether to protect the area as wilderness or lease it to oil companies for drilling.

Throughout human history, people have hunted animals such as these musk oxen in the arctic. The people who lived in the arctic depended on animals for food.

CHAPTER 1

A Place Called Time

▼

The meanings of some things are hard to explain. Try to explain the meaning of *time*. What is time? Is it a place? Is it a feeling? Is it something you can touch?

Can you imagine what the earth was like millions of years ago? Try to picture yourself living in a different time—maybe just a hundred years ago. And what will the earth be like in the future? As the old saying goes, "only time will tell."

One thing we can understand about time is that it is always moving. Time doesn't stand still. Seconds, minutes, hours, days, weeks, months, years, decades, centuries, ages—we are always measuring time! And as time passes, the world changes.

The earth is about six billion years old! That number seems beyond imagination. Humans have lived on the earth for just two million years. That is a long time, but not so long when compared to the age of our planet. The way we humans live has changed over time. And we have changed the earth!

In the beginning, people did not have much control over nature. We hunted animals and gathered plants for food. We lived in small groups and wandered great distances looking for good places in which to live and for plants and animals to eat.

Time Travel to an Industrialized World

Humans slowly learned how to do things that made life easier. We learned how to tame some animals to help us with our work, and we tamed other animals to use as food. The taming of wild animals and plants is called **domestication**. About twelve thousand years ago people learned how to plant wild seeds in gardens and grow the same plants year after year. The growing of crops for food is called **agriculture**.

Now that we could grow our own food, we had no reason to wander great distances. We settled in towns and cities and slowly our populations grew. These towns and cities were the first **civilizations**. Civili-

Modern agriculture has made it possible to grow enough food to feed large numbers of people in towns and cities.

zations are groups of people who live together and have written languages and laws to keep order.

As time passed, civilizations started all over the world. People invented machines to plow fields and guns to shoot animals. We built sailing ships and discovered new medicines. These are examples of **technology**.

Less than two hundred years ago, our technology began to change in important ways. We invented

Modern technology, such as the space shuttle, has changed the way people live and the way they view their world.

engines that were powered by fuel. This was the beginning of the **industrial revolution**. Engines started to do the work that animals, people, wind, and water had done.

Now our world is industrialized. Technology has solved many problems for us. Many diseases have been cured. People can travel all over the world with ease. We can grow huge amounts of food to feed large populations.

A Place from the Past?

But technology has created problems, too. Our land, water, and air are becoming polluted with industrial wastes. We are changing large areas of land to grow crops and build towns and cities. We are cutting down our forests to make buildings, houses, and paper. Many plants and animals are becoming **extinct**, or disappearing from the earth forever, because they have no place left to live. And we are drilling for oil in every corner of the world—oil that is used to run our cars and machines.

People today cannot go back to the time before technology changed the earth. But we can try to imagine places where people have never been. We can try to imagine what it was like to live on an earth that was wild and untamed by human hands. And we can ask, "Is there a place on earth that is the same now as it was thousands of years ago?"

CHAPTER 2

A Place Called Wilderness

▼

There is a place left on earth where time seems to have stopped. In this place animals run wild. Plants have not been trampled and cut to build roads and cities. Crops are not grown on the land for food. It is a place that has not been changed by human technology. Here most people live in some of the same ways as they have lived for thousands of years.

Welcome to the arctic wilderness! The arctic is a cold and harsh land found near the top of the world. It is the part of the world located closest to the North Pole. There is no land at the North Pole, only ice. It is so cold that the Arctic Ocean never melts there. This is why the North Pole is also called the polar ice cap.

There is no exact place where the arctic begins. Some scientists say it begins where trees can't grow. Others say it begins where the ground is frozen during all seasons of the year. And a third group says the arctic starts where people can no longer grow crops for food.

Land of the Midnight Sun

One way to see where the arctic begins is to look at a map and find the imaginary line called the **Arctic Circle**. Land north of the Arctic Circle has at least one day in summer when the sun never sets. It is sunny all night long. For the rest of the summer, the sun shines during most hours of the night. The arctic summer nights are called "white nights," because it is bright all night long.

Nights are "white" during arctic summers because the earth is tilted as it spins and circles around the sun. In summer, the northern part of the world (called the northern hemisphere) is tilted toward the sun. In the southern part of the world (the southern hemisphere) it is winter during this time because that part of the earth is tilted away from the sun.

As the earth makes its yearly journey around the sun, the northern hemisphere becomes tilted away from the sun during the winter months. The farther north a person travels the shorter daylight hours become.

During this time, the sun does not rise over the North Pole—it is dark all day long.

North of the Arctic Circle there is at least one day when the sun never rises. For the entire winter, it stays dark during most hours of the day.

The People

In this land of midnight summer sun, winter darkness, cold, and ice, some people have been able to survive over the centuries. For ten thousand years, people who call themselves the **Inuit**, have lived in the arctic. They are also called Eskimos.

The Inuit hunt animals for food. They depend on a northern deer, the caribou, for meat, clothing, and tools. They also hunt seals, walruses, polar bears, and birds. They fish in cold rivers for arctic char and other hardy fish.

Animals such as whales, seals, and walruses provide the Inuit with meat for food and oil to fuel their lamps and fires. They kill what they need for food, clothing, fuel, and tools and never let any part of an animal go to waste.

The Inuit sometimes do not have enough food

An Inuit man fishes for cod in the arctic.

during the long winters. But the Inuit people survived.
They learned how to live in the cold arctic wilderness.
They developed a **culture**, or way of life, much dif-
ferent from any other in the world.

Arrival of the Europeans

When explorers from Europe came to the Canadian
arctic in the late 1500s, they discovered a new land and
a new people. They named them Eskimos, a French
word meaning "raw-flesh eaters." The Europeans killed
many of the whales, walruses, and seals that the Inuit
depended on for food. The Europeans also brought
new diseases that caused many Inuit to die.

But the Alaskan arctic was still unexplored. Here the
Inuit and the animals they hunted still lived in the wilderness. Finally, in the 1800s, Europeans came to Alaska
to hunt whales, caribou, and other big animals. These
explorers and settlers hunted and killed every animal
they could find. The musk ox, a big and shaggy sheep
relative, was hunted until none were left in Alaska.

Still the Inuit did not give up their way of life.
Today they live differently than they did five hundred
years ago. Guns have replaced spears and boat motors

An Inuit boy in traditional clothing.

The Alaska pipeline.

have replaced oars. But many Inuit still depend on the wilderness for life.

The Discovery of Oil

Today all of the Alaskan arctic is not wilderness. In Prudhoe Bay, along the coast of the Arctic Ocean, oil was discovered in 1968. Now a huge pipeline, eight hundred miles long, carries oil from Prudhoe Bay to the port of Valdez, in southern Alaska.

Drilling for oil in Prudhoe Bay on Alaska's north slope.

Huge trucks travel on roads that crisscross the land along the coastline of Prudhoe Bay. The coastline has become polluted with chemicals from oil spills and drilling. These coastal lands no longer have ponds of clean water for wildlife to use. The fragile arctic plants that once lived there can no longer survive. The area around Prudhoe Bay is now a wasteland.

Already half the oil in Prudhoe Bay is gone. But there might be more oil that hasn't yet been drilled.

The Aufeiss Aichilik River in the Arctic National Wildlife Refuge.

Scientists think there is oil in the last stretch of wilderness that lies along the coast of the Arctic Ocean.

The Last Wilderness

In the northeast corner of Alaska is the biggest and the

last great piece of wilderness left in the United States. It is also one of the most important wilderness places left on earth. This is the Arctic National Wildlife Refuge (ANWR). The ANWR is more than nineteen million acres big—which is about the size of the states of Vermont, New Hampshire, and Massachusetts combined! Almost all of the ANWR is public land. This means it is owned by the United States government and by every American citizen.

The ANWR is a place where animals, plants, and the land itself are protected from humans. About eight million acres of the ANWR are actually protected as wilderness. Here no roads or houses or villages are allowed, and the only people are visitors.

But most of the ANWR is not protected as wilderness. This means the United States government can still let oil companies drill for oil in the ANWR.

If this happens, the ANWR will no longer be a wilderness. The Inuit may no longer have a place to hunt. And all Americans, all people, will lose one of the last places on earth that looks as it did thousands of years ago—when most of the world was wilderness.

CHAPTER 3

The Tundra

▼

Half of the Arctic National Wildlife Refuge is **tundra**. People of the Russian arctic named the treeless plains on which they lived the tundra. Now all arctic lands where trees cannot grow are known as tundra.

Tall mountains, the Brooks Range, divide the ANWR in two. On the southern slopes of these mountains are forests of spruce trees. On the northern slopes the tundra begins and spreads north to the shores of the Arctic Ocean. Few trees grow on the tundra because of the cold and windy climate. Trees that can survive the cold are very short: A hundred-year-old tree stands no taller than a small child!

During the summer the temperature stays cool—it averages about 50°F. The summer is short—only about eight weeks. Winter last for eight months! Because it is

The tall mountains of the Brooks Range divide the ANWR from east to west.

dark most of the winter, the temperature rarely rises above zero. It is also windy on the tundra. The wind makes the cold temperatures seem even colder, an effect called wind chill. The wind chill on the tundra sometimes makes the temperature fall to -100°F. or even colder!

Because it is so cold most of the year, the soil just below the surface of the tundra never completely thaws, or melts. Under the top layers of tundra plants and soil

Only short and very hardy trees grow on the tundra. These spruce trees may be fully grown, even old, although they are quite small.

is a thick layer of frozen ground called **permafrost**. The word *permafrost* is really two words combined: *permanent* and *frost*. Permafrost means the earth is permanently frozen, or frozen all the time.

In some places the ground has been frozen for

thousands of years. The thickest layer of permafrost in Alaska is 2,250 feet deep!

Besides being cold, the tundra is also a very dry place most of the year. In fact, it is a cold desert. It doesn't rain much during the summer, and there is little snow in the winter.

A Hard Place to Live

The tundra is a hard place for living things to survive. But many plants and animals do live on the tundra. All life on the tundra has similar problems. Plants and animals have ways of adjusting to the cold to keep from freezing in the winter. And they must **reproduce** and raise their young during the short summer when it is warm and there is enough food.

Animals and plants survive on the tundra because they have special **adaptations**. Adaptations are characteristics or traits that help a living thing survive in its surroundings. Some adaptations have to do with the way a plant or animal is made or shaped. For example, the polar bear is big, round, furry, and white. These are all adaptations to help it stay warm and blend in with its snowy surroundings.

The polar bear has adapted to life in the far north.

Other adaptations have to do with how an animal behaves or acts. For example, many birds fly from all over the world to lay their eggs on the tundra in spring. This behavior helps the birds survive because on the tundra there are no reptiles, which are animals that eat bird eggs.

Tundra plants also have adaptations. Mosses are plants that cover the tundra like a blanket but do not have roots and stems like most other plants. Without

In some places mosses cover the tundra like a blanket.

roots and stems, mosses cannot "suck" water out of the soil. Instead they get water from their tiny leaves, which soak up water from the ground. Mosses need a large and constant supply of water to survive.

But the tundra is a very dry place. How can mosses grow if there is not a lot of water? On the tundra, water from melting snow collects on the ground in the spring. Like a shield, the permafrost prevents water from sinking into the ground. During the summer, water sits on the surface of the tundra where it can be used by mosses and other plants and animals.

Two Plants in One!

Other common tundra plants are called **lichens**. Lichens look like bunches of crusty orange or green leaves growing on rocks. But they are different from all other plants. Lichens are really two kinds of plant that live together in a special relationship. One part of lichens are **fungi**.

Most plants can make their own food using energy from the sun. These are the green plants. Fungi are not green plants, and they cannot make their own food. Mushrooms and other fungi must get their food from the soil, or from other plants that have died.

On the tundra there is little soil on which fungi can grow. Fungi must grow on bare rocks where there is no food. The fungus, which makes up one part of a lichen, is "fed" by the other part—the **algae**. Algae are tiny plants that use energy from the sun to make food. The algae "feeds" the fungus and in return receives water and protection from the dry and cold climate. Neither algae nor fungi could survive alone on the tundra.

A puffball mushroom on the tundra.

Lichens are food for many animals on the tundra. Some animals eat lichens all year long because lichens do not die or wilt in the winter.

Keeping Warm

All the plants that live on the tundra are short and spread out over the ground. Mosses grow in clumps so they do not freeze to death in the winter. Lichens are tough plants that can survive the coldest temperatures.

Like the plants, only certain kinds of animals can live on the tundra. Most tundra dwellers are **warm-blooded.** Warm-blooded animals have a body temperature that never changes. People are warm-blooded: Our body temperature is usually 98.6°F.

There are two kinds of warm-blooded animals—the birds and the **mammals**. Birds have feathers to keep them warm, and they reproduce by laying eggs. Mammals have hair or fur to keep them warm, and their young are born alive after growing inside the mother. Young mammals are fed milk from the mother's body.

Most **cold-blooded** animals, such as amphibians (frogs, toads, and salamanders) and reptiles (snakes, turtles, and lizards) cannot survive on the tundra. The body temperature of cold-blooded animals changes with the temperature of the air. Most cold-blooded animals can't survive the extremely cold temperatures of the arctic winter.

But even on the tundra, some cold-blooded animals have adapted for survival. Insects are a group of cold-

Warble fly larvae grow on the back of this caribou.

blooded animals that survive in the arctic. Arctic bumblebees have adapted to the cold by storing a lot of fat in their bodies. Their thick, hairy "coats" also help to keep them warm.

Warble flies lay their eggs in the caribou's fur. The **larvae**, or wormlike young, live in the warm skin of the caribou all winter. By summer, they have grown to adult flies and the caribou shakes them out of its skin. The flies lay more eggs, and the life cycle starts again.

On the tundra, living things are **interdependent**—
that is, they depend on each other for survival. Every
living thing on the tundra is important. Mosses, lichens,
insects, birds, and mammals all need each other in ways
that are often hard to understand or see.

In the wilderness of the ANWR, time for repro-
ducing and growing is short. The midnight summer sun
comes and goes in two months. During that time, all
the animals and plants must prepare for the long winter
ahead.

CHAPTER 4

A Circle of Life

▼

Time in most places is like a circle. The seasons come and go and spring always comes back again. But some seasons on the tundra pass quickly. When spring arrives, it soon turns to summer, then fall. Winter arrives and stays for months and months. Life on the tundra has only a short time to reproduce and grow. And so it seems that life on the tundra—like time—is always moving.

Like time, living things have seasons—seasons for breeding, seasons for giving birth, seasons for growing, and seasons for resting. Some living things also move with the seasons. The arctic is a wilderness place where life moves across the tundra like waves on the ocean.

Caribou on the Move

The biggest movement of life across the tundra is the

migration of the caribou. Migration means movement from one place to another. And caribou are always on the move!

Caribou are big mammals related to deer. Traveling in large herds, they migrate across the tundra in search of food and places to have their young. Every year they follow the same routes or paths in the arctic.

Caribou eat plants. Lichens are their main food, but they also eat moss, grass, leaves, and mushrooms. Because lichens grow slowly, caribou must travel to new places to find plants that have not yet been trampled or eaten. Migration of the caribou gives the lichens a chance to grow back.

Almost two hundred thousand caribou migrate hundreds of miles across the Arctic National Wildlife Refuge every year. In spring, the caribou migrate to the northern part of the refuge.

This area is called the **coastal plain**. The coastal plain is a gently rolling stretch of tundra that runs along the shore of the Arctic Ocean.

The coastal plain is a **wetland**. This means the land is always wet, but not "drowned." The water is shallow enough for plants to grow above the surface. Wetlands

Caribou are large animals that depend on the plants of the tundra for food.

Viewed from the air, thousands of caribou migrate across the arctic coastal plain.

are very important places for wildlife. Many kinds of plants grow there that cannot grow in drier areas. Insects also need wetlands to breed and reproduce. Plants and insects are the main source of food for animals that migrate to the coastal plain.

The caribou use the coastal plain for **calving**, or giving birth to their baby calves. Mother caribou, called cows, give birth to one calf in late May or early June. Almost all the calves are born within a one-week period. This is an adaptation that protects the calves from **predators** (animals that kill and eat other animals for food) such as wolves. Wolves will not attack a calf if there are thousands of other cows and calves in the same area.

The baby calves are able to stand up and nurse from their mothers within one hour after they are born. The first twenty-four hours of a calf's life are very important. During this time the cow and the calf bond, or get to know each other. The calf and cow must know how to recognize each other's smell and sound. Sometimes cows and calves get separated while crossing rivers, and if they do not find each other quickly the calf will not survive.

During the summer, parts of the coastal plain are covered with swarms of mosquitoes. The mosquitoes breed and reproduce in the ponds of melted snow and ice water. Mosquitoes can suck a quart of blood from a caribou in one week! The caribou move toward the breezes along the ocean to escape the insects.

The cows are weak from their long journey and from giving birth. They need a lot of good food so their bodies can make milk for their newborn calves. Along the shores of the Arctic Ocean, they feast on arctic cotton grass, wildflowers, low-growing willow leaves, and other plants that are available only in the summer. These plants are rich in **nutrients** which help the caribou regain their strength. All the caribou must eat well so they will be strong enough to make their winter migration south.

By the middle of July, the caribou are ready to leave the coastal plain. They have given birth to their young and have fed on many kinds of plants. The young calves are strong and ready to migrate south to the foothills of the Brooks Range, or to places in Canada, to feed on lichens and shrubs during the long winter. When spring returns, the caribou will come again to the coastal plain.

Life of a Lemming

Other animals migrate across the tundra as well. Lemmings are small, mouselike mammals that live on the tundra and migrate short distances. In summer, lemmings live in wet areas where there is a lot of food. In winter, they move to drier areas where they live under the snow.

This flower in the pea family provides caribou with food during the short arctic summer.

Lemmings also have adaptations to help them survive during the summer and winter seasons. In summer their long claws work well for digging up plant roots to eat. But in the winter their claws change into flat pads. This adaptation helps them dig under the snow, where they live all winter.

Lemmings reproduce in the winter. Most animals and birds give birth to their young in the spring, when it is warm and there is plenty of food. But lemmings raise their young in tunnels under the ground.

Lemmings build their underground homes out of moss. Their underground tunnels protect them from the cold. There the lemmings are also protected from predators, such as the arctic fox. Lemmings are the **prey**, or food, for many larger mammals and birds.

In the spring, the tunnels become flooded with water from melting snow and ice. The lemmings can no longer live in their underground homes. During the summer the lemmings live on top of the tundra. The young lemmings that were born during the winter are big enough to find their own food and take care of themselves.

For three or four years, the lemmings live in the

The arctic fox is a predator that feeds on lemmings.

same area. More and more lemmings are born every winter. Then one spring arrives when there are too many lemmings and not enough food. All at once, large numbers of lemmings migrate across the tundra in search of food and a new place to live. Like the children who follow the Pied Piper in the fairy tale, one lemming leaves first, and the others soon follow!

The migrating lemmings are easily spotted by hungry predators. Snowy owls, hawks, foxes, wolves, and wolverines kill and eat most of the lemmings. The lemmings that escape find a new place to build their tunnels and reproduce.

It might seem strange that so many lemmings die during their search for a new and safe home. But this unusual adaptation helps lemmings survive. If lemmings did not migrate, *all* of them would die because they would run out of food.

A World of Birds

Birds also migrate. The tundra is a safe place for birds to lay eggs and raise young, because few predators on the coastal plain attack nesting birds. But there are plenty of plants and insects to feed on during the summer.

Some birds fly from as far away as South America—nearly twenty-five thousand miles—every spring! There are 108 different **species**, or kinds, of birds that come to the tundra from faraway places.

As soon as the ice melts, the birds arrive. They lay their eggs near the edges of small ponds on the coastal plain. The birds have three short months during

Snow geese migrate to the arctic coastal plain to lay eggs and raise their young.

which to lay their eggs, raise their young, and eat enough food to make them strong for their long migration to warmer climates!

Mosquitoes and other insects that hatch in swarms and drive the caribou to the ocean's edge are very important to birds. Without insects, birds would not have enough food on the tundra to survive.

The ducks, swans, and geese that make V shapes in the sky fly south in the fall. They will spend the winter feeding in warmer places such as California, Florida, and Mexico. In the spring they will return to the tundra to lay their eggs and hatch their young.

For some birds, the changing seasons are not as important. These birds live year-round in the arctic. The snowy owl is a big, fluffy, white bird. Snowy owls have thick feathers on their feet and can walk on the snow as if they were wearing snow shoes! In winter snowy owls are not easily seen because they blend in with the snow-covered tundra. Snowy owls eat lemmings and other small rodents.

Other year-round residents are the ptarmigans. These birds live inland. In winter their feathers are white like snow, but in summer they change to a brown color that blends in with tundra. This adaptation keeps them from being seen easily. Not all ptarmigans escape the view of predators. Throughout the winter and spring, ptarmigans provide food for the Inuit.

The Bearded Ones

The only large mammals that stay on the coastal plain during the winter are polar bears and musk oxen. Musk oxen were once a common sight on the arctic tundra.

Once almost extinct, musk oxen now live again in the ANWR.

But in the 1800s they were hunted and killed until none were left on the northern slope of Alaska. In 1969, sixty-nine musk oxen were brought to the ANWR from an island where they still lived. Since then, the musk oxen have reproduced, and now there are almost five hundred animals.

Musk oxen are big and shaggy. They are related to sheep. Their thick coats keep them warm in the winter. The Inuit call them *umingmak*, "the bearded ones."

Musk oxen eat grass—and a lot of it! Caribou and musk oxen can live side by side during the summer months because each animal eats different kinds of plants.

White Bears, Brown Bears

Polar bears are the only other big animals that live year-round on the coastal plain in winter. Most polar bears stay out on the ice packs of the Arctic Ocean. They live in dens during the winter and give birth to one or two tiny cubs in January. The cubs, which weigh less than two pounds when they are born, nurse from their mothers until spring. When they come out of their dens, they have grown to twenty-five pounds.

Sometimes a mother polar bear builds her den on land. The coastal plain, with its small hills, has good places to build snow dens. Wherever a mother builds her den, she must be close to the sea. In the sea live seals that polar bears eat.

Polar bears travel great distances throughout the arctic. They may even cross boundaries between different countries. For this reason, these large animals are protected by international laws. The only people who are allowed to kill polar bears are the Inuit, who use them for food and making tools.

Other bears live in the Arctic National Wildlife Refuge. Brown bears, or grizzly bears, follow the caribou to the coastal plain in the spring. Sometimes they kill caribou if they can catch one. Brown bears also eat plants, lemmings, and other small rodents. When the caribou leave the coastal plain in July, brown bears leave, too. They migrate south into the mountains of the Brooks Range, where they will spend the winter and give birth to their cubs inside warm dens.

Mammals of the Mountains

Other animals spend most of their lives in the mountains and foothills of the Brooks Range. Wolves, foxes, and wolverines are all predators. Dall sheep are sometimes the prey of wolves. These sheep stay on the northern slopes of the mountains, where there is less snow and more places to find plants to eat. The caribou return to the foothills and mountains to graze on lichens. There they, too, are preyed upon by wolves.

Running in Circles

In the Arctic National Wildlife Refuge, the changing

Dall sheep live in the Brooks Range of the ANWR.

seasons are an important part of life for every species
of animal and plant. Migration is one way animals adapt
to the changing seasons. These animals seem to live
their lives in circles, traveling from a summer home to a
winter home. They always arrive and leave at the same
time each year, as if they have clocks and calendars
built into their bodies!

Life in the arctic is always changing, never still. Life in the arctic seems magical, almost charmed. Through summers of midnight sunshine and long winters, animals, plants, and the Inuit survive in a delicate balance.

Far away from the Arctic National Wildlife Refuge, there is a different kind of movement that threatens this delicate balance. In our civilized world of cars, trucks, jet planes, factories, and cities, we are on the move all the time. Our movement is powered by oil—and there is oil in the ANWR.

CHAPTER 5

Wilderness or Oil?

▼

Time has always been important in the arctic wilderness. Short summers and long winters make survival possible for only the most well-adapted plants, animals, and people.

Now time has become important in another way. Time is running out for the United States Congress to decide if oil will be drilled in the Arctic National Wildlife Refuge. The most recent U.S. energy plan would open the ANWR for oil drilling.

If oil is drilled, what will happen to the lichens, the caribou, the polar bears, the birds, the lemmings, and the Inuit? If oil is drilled, how long will it last before it runs out? If oil is drilled, what will happen to one of the last great wilderness places left on earth?

Scientists, politicians, and the oil companies have been arguing about the answers to these questions for many years. Now the time is coming when a decision will have to be made. Either oil will be drilled or the entire Arctic National Wildlife Refuge will be protected.

Two Hundred Days of Oil

There is one chance in five that there is a lot of oil on the coastal plain of the ANWR. Scientists think there could be three billion barrels of oil beneath the coastal plain. It sounds like a lot of oil. But it takes Americans only two hundred days to use three billion barrels of oil.

Is two hundred days of oil worth the risk of damaging the coastal plain of the ANWR? The oil companies think they can drill the oil without hurting the plants and animals that live on or migrate to the coastal plain. They say it is possible to have both oil and wilderness. But many scientists disagree with the oil companies. They have studied other places in the arctic where oil has been drilled.

The Lost Tundra

For more than fifteen years, oil has been drilled in Prudhoe Bay, Alaska. Now the tundra at Prudhoe Bay is

After a huge oil spill in Alaska's Prince William Sound, a loon is
soaked with oil.

destroyed. Wastes from oil drilling have been dumped
on the tundra. And there have been many oil spills that
have leaked into the wetlands.

Animals and plants cannot survive in areas where
there have been oil spills. Sea mammals eat oil-covered
fish and die. Oil coats the feathers of birds and causes
them to drown. Oil seeps into bird eggs, killing the
young birds inside. Fish die when oily water gets into
their gills. Tundra plants cannot grow in the mud where

An oil-covered beach on Prince William Sound.

waste oil has been dumped. Without the tundra plants, caribou cannot survive. And predators such as wolves, grizzly bears, and the Inuit people will not have enough meat if caribou do not feed and reproduce on the coastal plain.

Pipeline to Disaster
The worst oil spill in American history happened on March 23, 1989, in Prince William Sound, Alaska. The

giant oil tanker the *Exxon Valdez* ran aground. The boat spilled ten million gallons of oil into the sea. An unknown number of fish, birds, and mammals died.

The oil that spilled into the sea was drilled at Prudhoe Bay. It was carried eight hundred miles across the tundra in a pipeline. If oil is drilled on the coastal plain of the ANWR, another pipeline will be built.

Tipping the Balance

The new pipeline will cut across the caribous' migration paths. Roads will be built, and towns for the oil workers to live in will be needed. All these things will disturb the delicate balance of life on the tundra in ways that scientists do not fully understand.

For example, thousands of snow geese migrate to the coastal plain to nest and feed. They must spend most of their time eating so they will be fat and strong enough for their long flight south. But when geese hear the noise made by airplanes, they get nervous and fly back and forth over the tundra. This extra movement burns up fat that is needed for their migration. If too much fat is burned, the geese cannot survive their long flight south.

A caribou herd in the Arctic National Wildlife Refuge.

Loud noises disturb other animals, too. If a mother polar bear hears a loud "boom" such as the sound that goes along with oil drilling, she will leave her den. A polar bear cub inside a den dies quickly once its mother is gone. Seals might be scared away by loud noises, and then polar bears would not have enough food.

No one knows for sure how the caribou herd would be affected by oil drilling. But scientists do know that caribou should not be bothered during the time they give birth to their calves. If the caribou are disturbed, cows and calves may not bond. This could cause calves to die during migration. The caribou might not eat enough food, and then they would not be strong enough to nurse the calves and migrate in winter.

All the calves are born on the coastal plain, close to where oil would be drilled. The coastal plain is their **habitat**, or living area, during the summer. The habitat includes all the things the caribou need to survive: food, water, protection, and enough space for raising their young. If the caribou habitat is destroyed, the herd cannot survive.

Many Inuit who live in the northern arctic depend on the caribou for their way of life. They eat caribou meat all year long. They make clothes out of caribou skins and tools out of antler and bone taken from caribou. The Inuit value the caribou as a gift that must be taken care of and respected. Without the caribou, the Inuit people could not survive in the arctic.

In the arctic there is no time for "mistakes." Animals cannot be disturbed during their short time on the coastal plain. If they are disturbed, their young may not live. Or they may not eat enough food to get them through the winter. Since all the animals and plants are interdependent, if just one is disturbed, they could all be affected.

A Short-Term Solution

Despite the threat to the wild animals and plants that live on the coastal plain, many people think drilling should be allowed. Even some of the Inuit people favor oil drilling because they say it will give them jobs and more money.

The oil companies say oil drilling should be allowed because the United States needs more oil. The U.S. government favors oil drilling because it would get money from the oil companies in return for letting them drill on land owned by the government.

But there are also many people who do not want oil drilled on the coastal plain. Most of the Inuit who live in northern Alaska and Canada do not want the coastal plain turned into an oil field. These people worry about how they will hunt the caribou if the animals no longer come to the coastal plain to feed and give birth. They worry about their land and water becoming polluted by the wastes dumped from oil drilling.

Saving for the Future

Conservationists are people who believe in protecting wilderness places and our environment. Conservationists say that the best way to increase our oil supply is not by drilling oil in the ANWR but by saving energy.

Energy can be saved in many ways. We all use energy every day, and most of our energy comes from oil. Turning out lights when they aren't really needed is a way to save energy. Turning our heat down in the winter saves energy. Installing insulation and new "super windows" prevents heat from leaking out of homes and other buildings.

The greatest energy savings can be achieved by driving cars less often. If people use car pools, use buses or trains more, drive cars that get better gas mileage, and ride bicycles and walk more, Americans would use much less oil. These are all ways to **conserve** energy. Conservationists estimate that the United States can cut its use of oil in half just by conserving energy. This is much more energy than what might be drilled from the Arctic National Wildlife Refuge.

There are other reasons to conserve energy besides trying to save wilderness places. Every time oil, gas, or coal—fossil fuel—is burned, **carbon dioxide** is released into the air. Carbon dioxide is an invisible gas that acts like a giant one-way mirror above the earth. The mirror of carbon dioxide lets in sunlight. But it prevents the heat from the sunlight from leaving the earth. Instead, the heat is trapped by the mirror of carbon dioxide and causes the earth to get warmer. This is called the **greenhouse effect**, because the earth gets hotter and hotter like the inside of a greenhouse.

Scientists think the greenhouse effect could raise the temperature of the earth enough to melt the ice at the poles. This could cause the oceans to rise and flood many of the coastlines around the world. Rising temperatures would also affect where crops can be grown. In some areas there could be major droughts that could cause a worldwide shortage of food.

To slow down the greenhouse effect, we must burn less fuel and find new sources of energy. **Solar energy** is energy taken from the sun. Scientists are studying ways to turn sunlight into electricity. Wind energy is another way to make electricity without burning fuel. If both of these kinds of energy are studied more, people will be able to use them in their everyday lives.

The Arctic National Wildlife Refuge is one of the largest wilderness areas left on earth.

Wilderness Is Forever

Many people that live far from the Arctic National Wildlife Refuge do not want oil drilled there. Most of them will never see the ANWR or even visit Alaska. But they want the ANWR **preserved**, or protected, because they believe there should be some places left on earth that are still wild and untouched by humans. These people know that once oil is drilled, the coastal plain will be forever changed. They say the Arctic National Wildlife Refuge was created to protect the animals and plants that live there. And they believe a few months' supply of oil is not worth destroying a wilderness place for all time.

Now the time has come for all Americans to make a decision about the ANWR and about other wilderness places. If we decide to save the coastal plain, we will be saving more than the caribou and polar bears. We will be saving part of times past, when most of the earth was wilderness. We will be giving a small piece of wilderness to future generations.

In today's modern world, if we hurt the land, the water, the air, and the living things we depend on, we are really hurting ourselves. Saving the wilderness is like making a promise to ourselves and to all the people who will come after us. It is a promise that life on earth will go on and that we will be a part of it.

Chapter 1: A Place Called Time

1. <u>Make a time line showing the history of people on the earth.</u> You will need a large piece of paper—two feet long and one foot wide (or several smaller pieces taped together), a ruler, a pencil, and crayons or colored markers.

a. First mark off two feet on the time line. Each foot represents one *million* years! At the very beginning of the time line write "THE FIRST HUMANS."

b. Divide the time line into inches. There will be twenty-four inches on your time line. Each inch represents about eighty-three thousand years.

c. In the space above the first twenty-three inches on the time line draw pictures of how people survived. Remember that these people hunted animals for food and gathered plants to eat. They did not live in one place.

d. The last inch on the time line represents the last eighty-three thousand years! Divide the inch into ten equal parts. On the second to last part, write "THE BEGINNING OF CIVILIZATION AND AGRICULTURE."

e. At the very end of the inch write "THE INDUSTRIAL REVOLUTION."

f. Now you can *see* how much people have changed in a very short time.

g. You can make other time lines showing shorter periods of time, too. This will help you see the events that have happened throughout the history of civilizations on earth.

2. <u>How much technology do you use?</u> Keep a diary for one day that keeps track of all the things you do that depend on technology. Remember that technology is using tools or machines to help solve problems or to accomplish something. You might include things like taking a bath, because you depended on pipes and a hot-water heater to give you warm water. Think about how you get and prepare your food. How do you stay warm? How do you travel from one place to another? How do you entertain yourself?

When you are done with your list, read it over carefully. Write a *U* next to the things you did that were unnecessary or not really needed for your survival. Put an *S* next to the things that you need to do to survive. Count the *S*s and *U*s. Do you do more things that are necessary or unnecessary for your survival?

Now look at your list again and decide which things you did that require a machine or something that runs on energy. For example, did you cook food that came out of a refrigerator? Both a stove and a refrigerator need energy to work. Put an *E* next to everything you did that required energy from electricity, oil, gas, or other fuel.

Is there anything on your list without an *E*? Maybe you wrote down *bike riding*. Riding a bike depends on technology because a bike is a machine. But bike riding does not require energy from a machine to make it go. The energy came from you. Write down *ME!* next to all the things you did that used only energy from your body—you may have written down *reading a book* or *playing ball*. If you are like most people, you will have mostly *E*s on your list! Try to think up ways you can use less technology and less energy in your everyday life.

Chapter 2: A Place Called Wilderness

3. <u>Write a haiku poem to describe your feelings about the wilderness.</u> Before you start, sit down and close your eyes. Try

to imagine what it is like in the arctic wilderness. Try to imagine what it is like in the summer, when the sun shines all night. Now imagine winter, with its cold winds and dark days. What would it be like trying to survive in the arctic wilderness? Imagine the animals and people that can survive there. What feelings do you have about the things you see in your imagination?

Now write your haiku poem. Haiku is a way of writing that was invented in Japan hundreds of years ago. Every word in haiku counts, because there are only seventeen syllables all together. A haiku poem should make a simple picture that causes the reader to feel an emotion or think about something. Here are the rules for writing haiku:

a. Haiku has seventeen syllables arranged in three lines: five syllables, seven syllables, then five syllables.

b. Write about something that you can see, not just something you feel.

c. Grammar and punctuation are up to you! You don't have to write complete sentences.

d. Try to write your poem in the present tense. This means to write it as if it is happening now (not in the past, and not in the future).

e. Tell just enough in your poem. Don't tell too much or too little. Some things should be left up to the imagination of the person reading the poem. Here is an example of a haiku poem (written by Issa, 1763-1829):

> Wild goose, wild goose
> At what age
> Did you make your first journey?

4. <u>Go to the library and find some books about the Inuit.</u> Read some of the legends or stories they told about the arctic and about the animals that they have shared their home with for

thousands of years. (One book you could borrow is called *Berry Woman's Children,* by Dale DeArmond, Greenwillow Books, New York.) Try to answer some of these questions:

How and why are animals important to the Inuit?

What do you think the word *wilderness* means to an Inuit child or adult?

Why are stories about animals so important to the Inuit?

Do you think you would like to live in the arctic as an Inuit child?

Try to write your own story about an animal that you like or are interested in.

Chapter 3: The Tundra

5. <u>Find out how many hours of sunshine there are in a day.</u> In the arctic, the sun shines most of the night during the summer. But in the winter it is dark almost all of the time. On the first day of fall and on the first day of spring, the days and nights are exactly the same length, no matter where you live. The first day of winter is the shortest day of the year (the least amount of sunshine), and the first day of summer is the longest day of the year.

You can see for yourself how the length of the days changes with the seasons by keeping a journal (which can be a calendar). On the first day of each month you should write down the time of the sunrise and the time of the sunset. You can find out the exact times by watching the daily weather broadcast on your local TV news show. Write down this information for the first day of each season, too.

You can see how the position of the sun above the earth affects the temperature by making a simple sundial. Take a yard-stick and plant it firmly in the ground in a place where it will not be moved for the entire year. Choose a time of the day when you will make your observations. (A couple of hours before or after noon is a good time to do this.) At the same time each day (on the first day of each month and season) measure the length of the shadow made by the yardstick. Also measure the temperature with a thermometer. Write down these numbers in your journal.

Does the shadow get longer or shorter as the summer turns to fall? Does the temperature get higher or lower as the shadow gets longer? What would your results be if you lived at the North Pole? What would your results be if you lived at the Equator?

6. <u>Invent an imaginary mammal that might be able to live in the arctic.</u> This project will help you understand how animals are adapted so they can survive in the environment in which they live. First make a list of some of the characteristics your animal will need by answering these questions:

How will your animal stay warm? (How long and thick is its fur? Is it a big or a small animal?)

How will your animal be protected from predators or hunters? (What color is its fur?)

What does your animal eat? (How long are its teeth? What is the shape of its mouth? Does it catch other animals with its claws, or other body parts?)

Does your animal live in one place, or does it migrate? (What kind of legs and feet does it have?)

When does your animal give birth to its babies? (Does it live in a den, a tunnel, or on top of the tundra?)

Now you can build your arctic animal! You will need these things: cardboard, scissors, glue, tape, string, buttons, cotton balls, markers, pipe cleaners, and colored felt.

a. First cut out the shape of your animal from the cardboard.

b. Glue on colored felt or cotton for fur.

c. Glue on buttons for eyes.

d. Make legs, a tail, teeth, and any other parts from pieces of felt, string, and pipe cleaners.

e. On an index card write the name you have given the animal and write a short story about how the animal lives.

Chapter 4: A Circle of Life

7. <u>Make an ARCTIC WILDLIFE CALENDAR.</u> This would make a nice gift for someone special! You will need at least thirteen pieces of paper (8 1/2" x 11" size), a ruler, colored markers, pencils or crayons, a hole punch, yarn or string, and another calendar showing the new year.

a. Start with January. With the ruler make boxes for the days of the week. Number each box with the days of the month. You can add things like the phases of the moon if you want to and holidays like New Year's Day and Martin Luther King's birthday.

b. On a separate sheet of paper do the same for every month of the year. Make a cover sheet for your calendar showing the year. Arrange the papers in the correct order, from the cover to December. Make three holes along the top edge of the papers and string them together with yarn or string.

c. Now comes the fun part! Draw a picture of the arctic on the cover with the year the calendar is for. Turn the page when you're finished. Now on the back side of the cover, you will draw a picture for January.

d. Draw a picture for January to show what is happening during that month in the arctic. What happens in the arctic during January? Some things you could include are polar bears giving birth to their babies inside their snow dens; grizzly bears having their babies; lemmings having many babies in their underground tunnels; caribou in the foothills of the mountains, eating lichens; snowy owls and ptarmigans hunting for small rodents on the tundra.

e. Read over the list below for each month and draw a picture to match each month. When you are finished you will have a calendar of arctic wildlife!

February: It is still dark most of the day, but it is getting brighter. Polar bear and grizzly bear cubs nurse from their mothers and are growing bigger. Lemmings give birth to their young in underground tunnels.

March: The first day of spring is usually March 21. There are exactly twelve hours of daylight and twelve hours of darkness on the first day of spring. After this day, the days will get longer and longer. In late March, baby polar bears come out of their dens with their mothers. Wolves mate in March.

April: Polar bears move onto the sea ice to feed on seals. Grizzly bears come out of their winter dens.

May: Wolves give birth to their young inside dens. Caribou arrive on the coastal plain. Grizzly bears also come to the coastal plain. The Inuit hunt caribou, mostly in the spring and summer.

June: The snow has finally melted, and the ice along the shore has melted. Most of the caribou give birth to their calves during the first week in June. Swans and ducks arrive and lay their eggs next to ponds. The first day of summer is usually June 21. This day is the longest day of the year around the world. In the arctic, the sun never sets! The tundra is in full bloom, with hundreds of types of wildflowers.

July: Mosquitoes and other insects have hatched and drive caribou to the ocean's edge. Caribou feed on grasses, mosses, and lichens. The grizzly bears leave the coastal plain because the caribou have moved. Lemmings migrate and provide food for many birds like owls, hawks, and eagles.

August: The caribou leave the coastal plain and begin their migration south. Swans begin their migration south. The days are getting shorter, and it is getting colder. Snow geese arrive from their northern breeding grounds to feed on the coastal plain before continuing south.

September: The first snows fall, and the swans, geese, and ducks leave the arctic for warmer climates. Grizzly bears build their dens near the mountains. The first day of fall is September 21. There are twelve hours of sunshine and twelve hours of darkness. After this day, the sun will shine for fewer and fewer hours during the day.

October: Polar bears move to the land to look for places to build dens. Ice covers all the ponds, and the water along the shore is freezing.

November: Polar bears build dens and sleep inside, awaiting the birth of their cubs. Musk oxen remain on the coastal plain, even though it is very cold and windy.

December: The first day of winter is December 21. This is the shortest day of the year. In the arctic, the sun never rises! The tundra seems to be asleep under a blanket of snow and ice. But in underground tunnels, lemmings keep warm! Inuit hunt ptarmigans on the tundra.

8. <u>Show how animals and plants in the arctic are inter-dependent by making a giant food web.</u> A food web is a group of food chains connected together. A food chain is the way food is transferred between plants and animals. For example, a simple food chain is a plant, which is eaten by an insect. The insect is eaten by a bird. And the bird is eaten by a mammal. Food webs are formed when food chains overlap.

To make your food web you will need index cards, colored string or yarn, a bulletin board, thumb tacks, and crayons or markers. Draw pictures of plants and animals on the index cards. Make food chains by connecting the cards with string and tacking them to a bulletin board. Make a food web by connecting the food chains with different-colored string or yarn.

Here are some simple food chains to get you started. See if you can figure out how to connect them to make a food web.

Arctic cod fish→seals→polar bears

lichens→caribou→wolves, grizzly bears, Inuit

left-over dead caribou parts→foxes, wolves, ravens (birds)

plant roots→lemmings→snowy owls

caribou blood→insects→birds

eggs of sea birds→auks (a kind of bird)→Arctic fox

Chapter 5: Wilderness or Oil?

9. <u>Do an experiment to find out what happens to birds after an oil spill.</u> You will need these things: some hard-boiled eggs (at least three), used motor oil, bird feathers, a shallow bowl or other container, cooking oils, food coloring, and a magnifying glass.

a. Put some used motor oil in a shallow bowl. (Do not use a bowl you eat from. A good container for this experiment can be made by cutting the bottom out of an old plastic milk or larger laundry-detergent container.)

b. Put the eggs into the oil. Using protective gloves, such as rubber gloves, take one out after five minutes. Try to get the oil off the egg by washing it in water. Peel the shell off the egg. What do you see? Cut into the egg. What do you see?

c. Take the second egg out of the oil after fifteen minutes. Try to wash the shell, and do the same as above.

d. Take the third egg out of the oil after thirty minutes. Do the same as above.

e. Try the same experiment with other oils (cooking oils). If the oil does not have color to it, add food coloring so you can see the effects it will have on the eggs.

Answer these questions:

What did the eggs look like inside after being soaked in oil?

Does it matter how long the egg stayed in the oil?

Why can't you wash the oil away with water?

What effect would an oil spill on the coastal plain have on the birds that nest and raise their young there?

Which kind of oil causes the most damage to the eggs? Why?

Now try some experiments with feathers. First look at a feather with a magnifying glass. Draw a picture of what you see. Then dip the feather in some oil for a couple of minutes. Look at it with the magnifying glass and draw a picture of what you see. Try to wash the oil off with water. What happens?

Answer these questions:

What does oil do to feathers?

Do you think birds with oil-covered feathers can fly?

Can they swim?

Will the oil ever wash out of the feathers?

10. <u>Conserve energy!</u> Here are some easy ways you can save energy every day.

a. If everybody turned his or her heat down by six degrees in the winter, we would save half a *million* barrels of oil every *day*! You can turn your heat down and still be warm enough by wearing a sweater inside! Turn your heat down by five degrees and put on a warm sweater and socks. If you get too warm after half an hour, then turn your heat down some more. Keep adjusting the heat lower until you find a temperature you are comfortable with when wearing a warm sweater!

b. There are many places in a house from which heat escapes. At night a lot of energy is wasted when people don't close their shades and curtains. Make sure all the curtains and shades are closed at night and on very cold days. Check your home for "heat leaks." On a cold day, take a strip of paper and put it against places in doors and windows where you think heat is escaping. If the paper moves a little bit, then you have found a leak. Write down all the places that have heat leaks and show the list to your parents. Together you can fix the leaks with caulking and weatherstripping that is available at the hardware store.

    c. It takes a lot of energy to heat water. When you take a shower or bath, try to use less hot water. Turn off the faucet as soon as you are finished washing your hands or face.

    d. Lights also use energy. Turn out the lights when no one is in the room. If it is sunny outside, open the curtains to let the sunshine in. Dusty, dirty light bulbs use more energy than clean bulbs, so clean off your light bulbs once in a while. You can save a lot of energy by changing the kind of light bulbs you use. *Fluorescent light bulbs* use one quarter the energy as regular light bulbs. You can find these at hardware stores.

    e. Appliances like ovens, refrigerators, TVs, and radios all use energy to work. Save energy by closing the refrigerator door quickly, covering pots when cooking or boiling water, and turning off the TV and radio when nobody is watching or listening.

    f. It takes energy to make packaging and other materials. Try to recycle as many things as you can. Separate your trash, and save cans, bottles, jars, newspapers, and any other materials that can by recycled.

    g. Ride your bike or walk everywhere you can, instead of having your parents drive you. Start a journal in which you write down the date, where you rode or walked, and how many miles you went. Challenge a friend or brother or sister to do the same. See who can go the most miles in each month of the year.

    11. <u>If you do not want oil drilled in the Arctic National Wildlife Refuge, you can help!</u> You can write a letter to your

congressmen and -women. You can even write to the president! Tell your friends and family about the ANWR and ask them to write letters, too.

When you write your letter, try to keep it short but to the point. Tell your senators, representatives, and the president that you are a young person who wants the coastal plain of the Arctic National Wildlife Refuge to be left a wilderness place. Tell them you care about the future of our earth and you think the wilderness is important for future generations. Ask them to support legislation or laws that will protect the ANWR from oil drilling and that will help our country save more energy.

This is how to address and mail your letters:

> The Honorable [name of representative]
> U.S. House of Representatives
> Washington, D.C. 20515

> The Honorable [name of senator]
> U.S. Senate
> Washington, D.C. 20510

> The Honorable [name of the president]
> The White House
> Washington, D.C. 20500

Environmental Groups Working to Protect the ANWR

Here is a list of some of the organizations that are working to protect the Arctic National Wildlife Refuge from oil drilling. You can write to them to learn more about what they are doing. You may also become a member of a group. By doing so you will be helping to preserve the ANWR.

The Alaska Center for the Environment
519 West 8th Avenue, Suite 201
Anchorage, AK 99501

The Alaska Coalition
330 Pennsylvania Avenue, S.E.
Washington, D.C. 20003

National Audubon Society
645 Pennsylvania Avenue, S.E.
Washington, D.C. 20003

National Wildlife Federation
1412 Sixteenth Street, N.W.
Washington, D.C. 20036-2266

Northern Alaska Environmental Center
218 Driveway
Fairbanks, AK 99701

Sierra Club
730 Polk Street
San Francisco, CA 94109

The Wilderness Society
1400 Eye Street, N.W.
Washington, D.C. 20005

Glossary

▼

adaptation—characteristic, trait, or behavior that helps a plant or animal survive in its environment.

agriculture—the growing of crops for food.

algae—a one-celled plant that can make food from the sun's energy.

Arctic Circle—an imaginary line that marks the place on earth where there is at least one complete day of sunlight and one complete day of darkness during the year.

calving—giving birth to baby calves.

carbon dioxide—an invisible gas released into the atmosphere when fossil fuels are burned. Carbon dioxide forms a shield, like a one-way mirror over the earth, which lets sunlight in and doesn't let heat out.

civilization—the grouping of people in towns and cities where there is written language, laws, and agriculture.

coastal plain—the stretch of tundra that runs along the shore of the Arctic Ocean.

cold-blooded—an animal that has a changing body temperature depending on the temperature of the air.

conservationists—people who believe that the earth's resources should be protected and cared for.

conserve—to save for the future.

culture—the way of life a group of people has developed over thousands of years.

domestication—the taming of wild animals and plants to be raised or grown as food or for work.

extinct—no longer living anywhere on earth.

fungi—plants that cannot make their own food from the sun's energy. They get food from other dead plants.

greenhouse effect—the warming of the earth due to the increase of carbon dioxide in the atmosphere.

habitat—the area where an animal or plant naturally lives and everything it needs for life. Habitat includes food, water, shelter, and enough space to reproduce and raise young.

industrial revolution—the change from people and animals as the main source of energy to the use of machines and engines to do work. The invention of engines that burn fossil fuels was the beginning of the industrial revolution.

interdependent—the way animals and plants depend on each other, or need each other, for survival.

Inuit—the people who have lived in the arctic for thousands of years (sometimes called Eskimos).

lichen—a plant made of fungi and algae. The fungi provides protection and the algae makes food.

mammals—warm-blooded animals with fur or hair on their bodies. They give birth to live young and nurse their young.

migration—the movement of animals from one place to another in search of food or places to give birth.

nutrients—the parts of food that help a living thing grow.

permafrost—the permanently frozen layer of ground beneath the soil in the arctic.

predator—an animal that hunts and kills other animals for food.

preserved—saved or protected from destruction.

prey—an animal that is hunted and killed by other animals.

reproduce—to make more of the same species; to give birth.

solar energy—the energy that comes directly from the sun.

species—a group of animals or plants that are alike. Members of the same species can breed and reproduce to make seeds, eggs, or young.

technology—a way to use knowledge and science to solve problems and make things people use. Tools and machines are examples of technology.

tundra—the treeless land found mostly above the Arctic Circle.

warm-blooded—animals that always have the same body temperature, regardless of the surrounding temperature.

wetland—land that is always wet, but where the water is shallow enough for plants to grow.

wilderness—a place where humans do not live but are just visitors. There are no roads, buildings, or towns in the wilderness.

Index

▼